N

7,214 km (4,483 mi.)
northwest to Hawai'i

6,930 km (4,306 mi.)
west to New Zealand

W

E

3,540 km (2,200 mi.)
east to Chile

S

Rapa Nui (Easter Island)

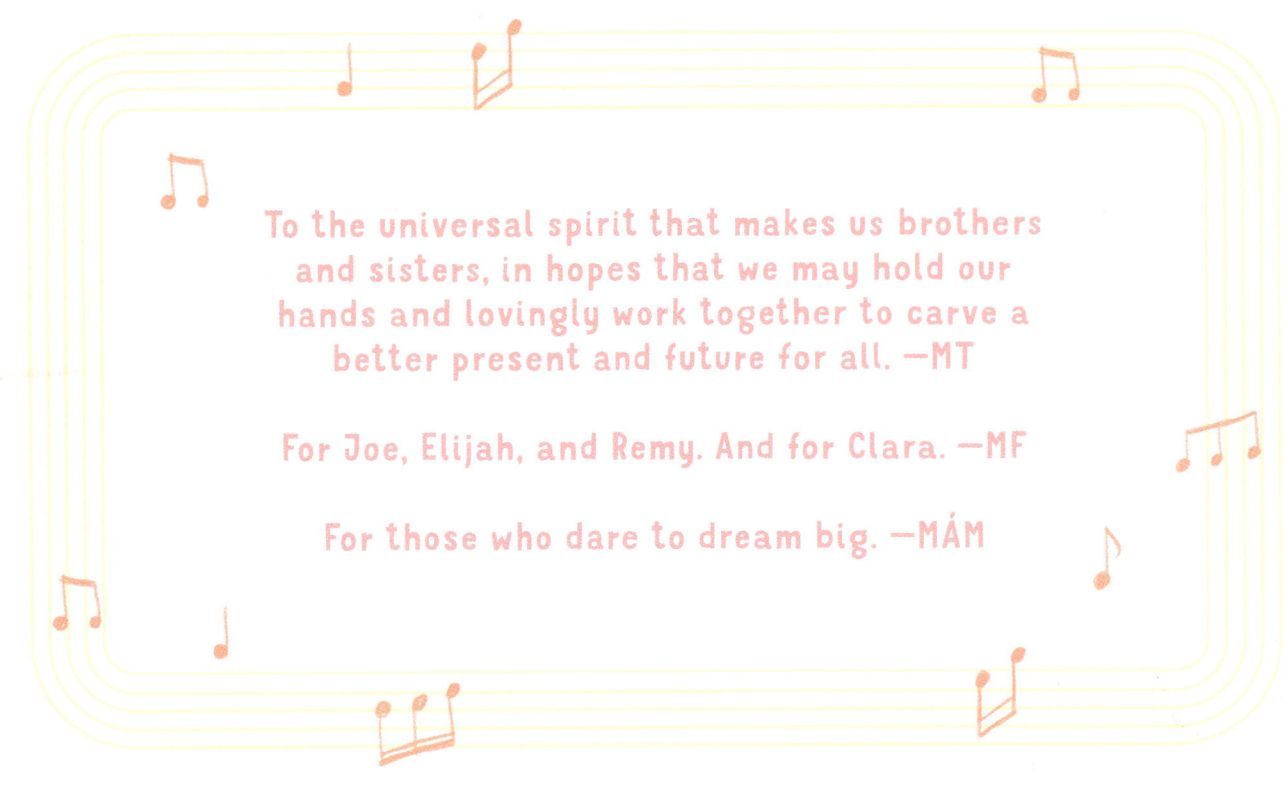

To the universal spirit that makes us brothers and sisters, in hopes that we may hold our hands and lovingly work together to carve a better present and future for all. —MT

For Joe, Elijah, and Remy. And for Clara. —MF

For those who dare to dream big. —MÁM

Text © 2023 by Mahani Teave
Text by Marni Fogelson
Illustrations © 2023 by Marta Álvarez Miguéns
Cover and internal design © 2023 by Sourcebooks

Sourcebooks and the colophon are registered trademarks of Sourcebooks.

The full color art was painted digitally.

Published by Sourcebooks eXplore, an imprint of Sourcebooks Kids
P.O. Box 4410, Naperville, Illinois 60567-4410
(630) 961-3900
sourcebookskids.com

Cataloging-in-Publication Data is on file with the Library of Congress.

Source of Production: Wing King Tong Paper Products Co. Ltd., Shenzhen, Guangdong Province, China
Date of Production: October 2022
Run Number: 5027184

Printed and bound in China.
WKT 10 9 8 7 6 5 4 3 2 1

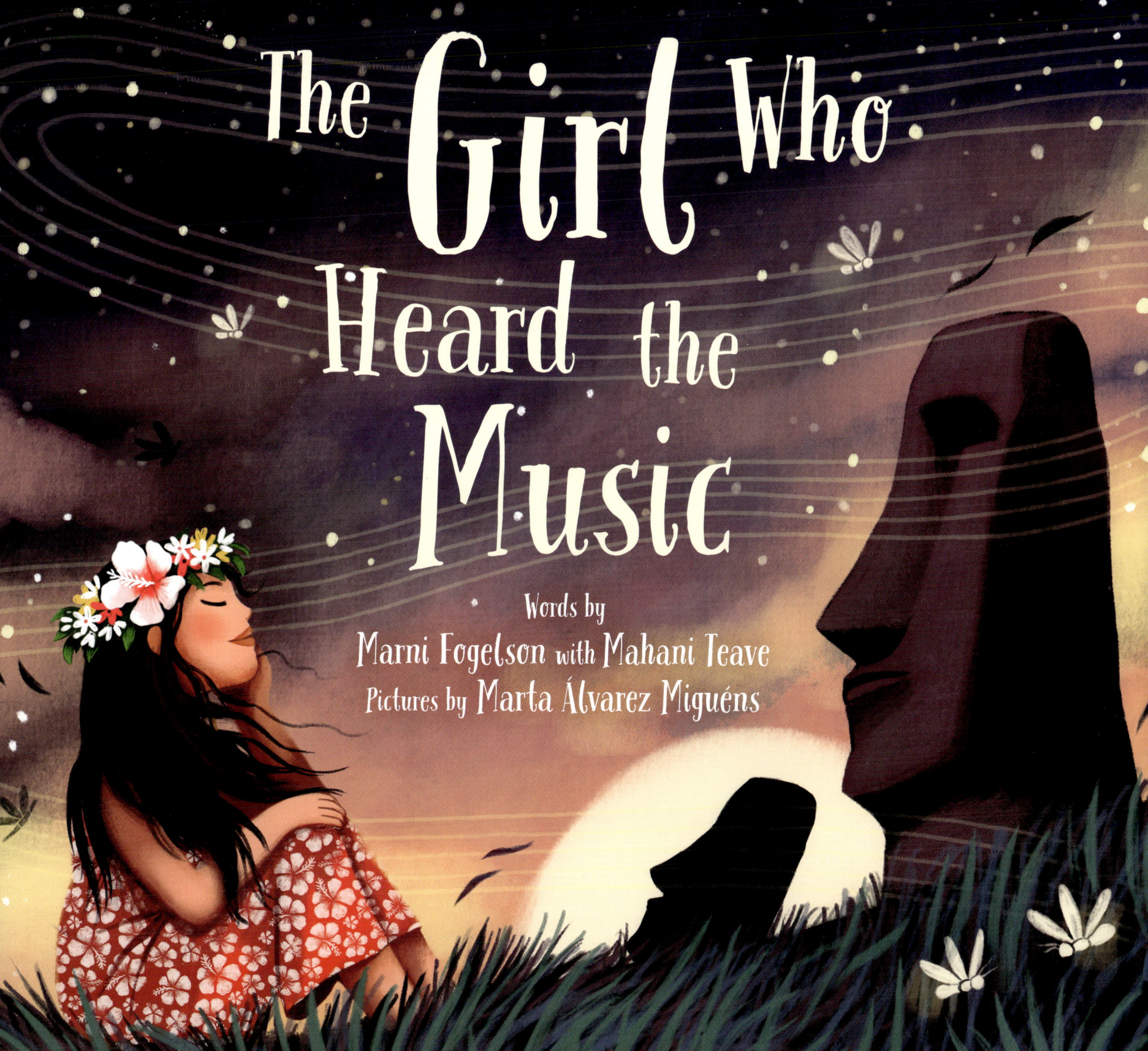

The Girl Who Heard the Music

Words by
Marni Fogelson with Mahani Teave
Pictures by Marta Álvarez Miguéns

sourcebooks
eXplore

On Rapa Nui, a small island that is watched over by giant statues called moai, it seemed to a little girl named Mahani that music was everywhere.

From the lullabies that mothers sang, to the rhythm of the waves hitting the rocks, to the crickets calling to each other at dusk, music was the heart, the *inaŋa*, of Rapa Nui.

Sometimes, visitors to Rapa Nui gave the children music lessons. Classical music sounded different from the ukeleles and songs Mahani knew. She fell in love with the way it made her feel…and her fingers itched to play the instruments she heard.

When those visitors left, they also took their instruments and the rest of their knowledge.

Every time Mahani had to say goodbye, her heart drooped like a tipanie flower past its prime.

When Mahani was nine, a retired music teacher arrived in Rapa Nui with a piano. A real piano! It was the only piano on all of Rapa Nui, and Mahani pleaded for the chance to learn.

In the teacher's living room, Mahani practiced the notes…until one day, *click*!

Mahani looked at the sheet of music before her and realized she could read it all, each and every note.

After her lesson, Mahani zoomed down the hill to her house on her bicycle, her joy overflowing like bursts of hibisco blossoms.
"I can play ANYTHING now," Mahani thought.
(Well, almost.)

Sadly, the teacher's visa soon expired and she had to leave too.

Another visitor, a great Chilean pianist, also heard Mahani perform. He was astounded that Mahani had only been playing for a few months. He knew that her talent could not fully bloom if she stayed on Rapa Nui.

It was hard for Mahani to leave the flowers and the crickets and the moai on the island she loved.

But just like her ancestors who were courageous explorers, Mahani voyaged into the unknown. She left the island.

Mahani studied at conservatories around the world. She won international competitions. She played at concert halls, schools, hospitals, and jails. Music, she believed, belongs to everyone.

As she played for audiences across six continents, Mahani kept Rapa Nui close to her heart. To feel at home on stage, she often wore flowers in her hair.

When Mahani would come back home, she could never stay long. There wasn't even a piano on the island for her to play anymore! But the magic and music of Rapa Nui made Mahani feel whole again.

Rapa Nui always had visitors, but word spread about the island's amazing moai and natural beauty. Soon, more than a hundred thousand tourists were finding their way to Rapa Nui every year.

Mahani noticed that something else was
finding its way to her homeland.
Trash
was
everywhere.

The vibrant blue water around Rapa Nui acts like a
vortex, trapping ocean litter and lining the beaches with it.
And the tourists leave behind tons of garbage—too much
for the island's only landfill.

Rapa Nui is a small island. But it was in big trouble.

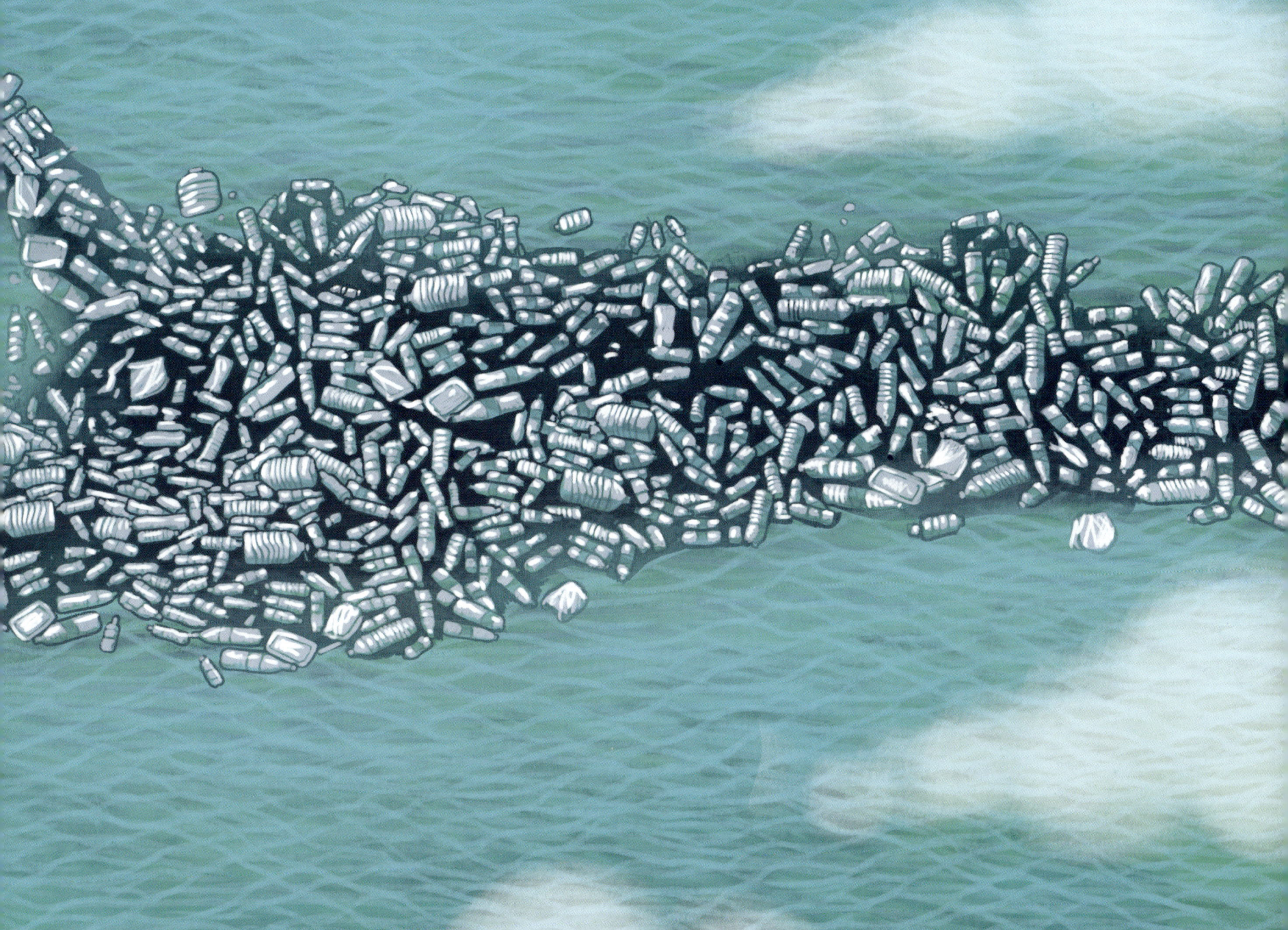

One day, while watching the light from the setting sun kiss the moai's magnificent faces, Mahani thought about how much work it had taken to carve the statues long ago with rock tools called *toki*.

Carving a new future for the island would take a lot of work too. But she would help!

Mahani joined a group of islanders who had ideas for Rapa Nui's future too. Like the keys on a piano playing in harmony, the team worked together on a shared dream: to build the island's first music school!

Just as her ancestors used toki to turn volcanic ash into moai, Mahani and her team discovered a way to transform the trash polluting their island. They would build with it!

With the help of volunteers from around the world, they constructed the school, using approximately:

12 tons of cardboard
40,000 aluminum cans
25,000 glass bottles
20,000 plastic bottles
2,500 tires

More than 7 years of garbage now lives in the school's walls!

When the school was finally finished, they celebrated all of the hard work in the perfect way: with a concert!

Although the Rapa Nui School of Music and the Arts was made with tons of trash, it's powered by nature! Solar panels turn energy from the sun into electricity, and giant barrels hold rainwater for gardens.

Now piano and cello music mix with ukulele and voices singing *re'o riu*. The children practice traditional *ori* and *hoko* steps as they go to and from their lessons.

The gardens grow fruits and vegetables so the island can depend less on food from other places. Mahani hopes the land will be reforested and treated with the same respect her ancestors gave it.

Music is still everywhere on Rapa Nui, and now there are new voices and sounds alongside the old.

Mahani carries this music with her wherever she goes, even to concert halls and recording studios on the other side of the world.

Meanwhile, pieces of Mahani's dream and her inaŋa remain on Rapa Nui. They continue to bloom on this wondrous island where she first heard the music.

Growing up on the island of Rapa Nui, Mahani Teave learned to appreciate the overwhelming power of nature from the expansive ocean views to the blackest skies full of glittering stars. But despite her home's far-flung location, she never felt isolated. It was her whole world and still felt big.

When she was nine years old, Mahani wrote a letter to the Chilean pianist Roberto Bravo, who visited the island and heard her play. Bravo was impressed with her talent and encouraged her to keep developing her craft. She left the island to study at prestigious conservatories with acclaimed teachers Ximena Cabello, Sergei Babayan, and Fabio Bidini. Mahani began performing all over the world as a concert pianist, but interrupted this blossoming music career to return to her island home and co-found NGO Toki, a nonprofit dedicated to the island's cultural and ecological preservation. Mahani now also works as a cultural ambassador and humanitarian. She hopes the school can serve as a model for other regions around the world and that her story will inspire people to share more love and empathy, play more music, and work together to mitigate climate change.

NGO Toki emerged from the shared dream of a group of Rapanui friends: to protect the island and people through the legacy of their ancestors. The Rapa Nui School of Music and the Arts has given hundreds of children lessons in piano, violin, cello, orchestra, and music theory. The school also teaches Rapa Nui traditions including ancient song, dances, ukelele, carving, and body painting, and these teachings help strengthen connections to the Rapanui language.

Co-founder Enrique Icka donated his land for the school and headed a team of volunteers from around the world to construct the building. Juan Haoa leads a project to increase production from Toki's organic gardens and greenhouses, using a combination of ancestral and modern agricultural techniques, and is sharing this knowledge with the community. On the world's most isolated inhabited island, food sovereignty is an important issue and a goal that Toki is working toward. To learn more about all of Toki's founders, programs, and mission, visit **Tokirapanui.org**.

Mysterious Moai

- The Moai are megalithic statues carved from concentrated volcanic ash and placed on ceremonial platforms called *ahu*.
- On Rapa Nui they are known as *ariŋa ora*, the living faces of the ancestors. The moai were likely first created around six hundred years ago to honor ancestors and past chiefs.
- There are eight hundred moai on Rapa Nui and each one is different.
- The average moai is over thirteen feet tall and weighs about fourteen tons!
- Scholars debate exactly how the Rapanui moved the massive moai from the volcanic craters where they were carved to the places where they now stand. Island legend claims they walked there using supernatural powers called *mana*.

Rapanui Language

The Rapa Nui School of Music and the Arts seeks to protect it by teaching it to young people there. Here are a few Rapanui words, ancient and contemporary:

- **'lorana:** hello and goodbye
- **māuru-uru:** thank you
- **mo'a:** respect to one's self and to everything around us
- **umaŋa:** to work together, to collaborate
- **inaŋa:** heart
- **riu:** ancestral song
- **toki:** carving tool

Island Facts

- Rapa Nui is also known as Easter Island, after Dutch explorers landed there on Easter in 1722. But people had already been living on Rapa Nui for hundreds of years by then.
- Rapa Nui has been a part of Chile since 1888, even though it's over two thousand miles away.
- Around eight thousand people live on Rapa Nui year-round, but more than a hundred thousand tourists come each year.
- It's considered one of the most remote inhabited places on Earth. The nearest inhabited land is Pitcairn Island, 1,289 miles away.

Earthships

The Rapa Nui School of Music and the Arts is an Earthship. Architect Michael Reynolds pioneered this kind of building in the 1970s and he traveled to Rapa Nui to show the Toki team how to build one. Some facts about Earthships:

- They're constructed with natural materials as well as recycled things—like tires!
- They have built-in renewable energy sources like solar panels or windmills.
- Roofs are designed to collect rainwater to use as an additional water source.
- Gardens for growing food are a part of every Earthship.
- There are about three thousand Earthships across the world.

Plastic in the Ocean

Plastic makes up 80 percent of today's ocean garbage, and these traveling pieces of trash are dangerous to animals. Some turtles and birds mistake plastic bags for food, while fish and other sea animals ingest the microscopic plastic pieces that remain after bags and bottles break down in the ocean. Some scientists believe that by 2050, ocean plastic might outnumber fish!

The Future of Rapa Nui

Rapa Nui faces many environmental challenges, such as land erosion, threatened water sources, the extinction of animal and plant species, and the many tons of garbage generated every year. But the people of Rapa Nui are taking action. The Rapa Nui Marine Protected Area keeps endangered species safe from mining and industrial fishing. Community groups are also reforesting, planting gardens, and organizing trash pickups. The island aims to be sustainable and waste-free by 2030.